KNOWING JESUS

Knowing
JESUS

moving beyond academics into intimacy

NRJOHNSON

◇ deeperChristian Press

Knowing Jesus
© 2015 by NRJohnson

Published by deeperChristian Press
PO Box 654 | Windsor, CO 80550

Printed in the United States of America

ISBN-10: 069237907X
ISBN-13: 978-0692379073

deeperChristian.com

*This ministry is maintained by the Lord
through the stewardship of those who value it.*

Knowing Jesus

moving beyond academics into intimacy

INTRODUCTION

If someone asked you if you know Jesus, how would you respond? If you were to summarize your relationship with Jesus in five words, which ones would you choose?

In fact, why don't you do that right now? Spend a moment in prayer and think about how you would honestly describe your relationship with Jesus. Write the words down somewhere or use the space below.

1. _____

2. _____

3. _____

4. _____

5. _____

Take a step back and look at the five words you chose. Why those words? Do they convey excitement, passion, and a growing intimacy with Jesus ... or do they seem more stoic and academic in nature?

Too often our relationship with Jesus consists of little more than attending a church service on Sundays, memorizing Bible stories, and spending fifteen minutes each morning in prayer and reading. We say we know Jesus, but if someone measured our intimacy with Him in a manner similar to how you would talk about a marriage, our knowledge of Christ would be akin to having a picture of our spouse to look at and knowing all the important details but failing to actually spend time with the person.

Knowing Jesus is more about relationship than rhetoric and more about intimacy than information.

In this short book, I want to examine a passage in Philippians 3 in which Paul talks about his own personal relationship with Jesus and what it means to actually know Christ. But to lay the foundation for what Paul says, let me start by telling you a story from my childhood to show how my early years brought me to the place where I long to know Jesus more and more.

THE EARLY YEARS

When I was a little kid I had a desire for money. I loved to hear the jingle of coins in my pocket, and I loved the green stuff in my camo-colored, velcro wallet. And so somewhere around age six or seven, I came up with a brilliant idea—I needed to make money. However, there is only so much a little kid can do.

In a moment of epiphany I ran to my mom and begged her to make a pitcher of lemonade. While she whipped up the yellow liquid that I was going to convert to gold, I ran downstairs to our craft room, grabbed a poster board, and sprawled with huge, kid letters:

Lemonade 10¢

I just knew this was going to be the secret to my success!

I pulled an old card table out to the street corner, stuck my sign on the front, thanked my mom for the lemonade, and snatched a mile-high stack of paper cups from the pantry, convinced I was going to sell out in under an hour.

The problem was that our house was in the back of a neighborhood ... which was nestled in the back of a bigger residential community. Basically, we didn't get much traffic—great for a family with small kids; bad for my entrepreneurial endeavors.

After what seemed like half of my little-kid life (which was probably more like twenty minutes), I decided that if I was going to have my shot at being a millionaire, I was going to have to take some risks. And that's when I crafted "the plan."

The plan was rather simple: whenever people were walking down the sidewalk in front of our house, I would jump in front of them and explain that they could not pass unless they gave me ten cents ... and in exchange they could not only pass, but take a glass of incredible, homemade lemonade (straight from the store packet, mixed with water and sugar by the loving hands of my mother). What more could someone ask for?

And the plan started to work!

In fact, it worked so well that I crafted phase two of "the plan." Now whenever someone rode their bike down the sidewalk, I would jump out in front of them and give them the same "do not pass" routine until I got my money. Let me clarify— this wasn't a "big bully" intimidation routine, but basic economics—they got a great glass of lemonade, and I got a pocket full of dimes ... they just didn't know they wanted the lemonade until I forced them to stop and realize how thirsty they were.

Phase two worked so well that I devised my most brilliant plan of all. We didn't have a lot of traffic in our neighborhood, so I decided that every time a vehicle drove by I would jump out in front of the car and give them the same opportunity to buy my lemonade. Hey, if the lemonade was really THAT good, why wouldn't everyone want some?

• • • • •

A few years later I realized that I needed to expand my horizons. I gathered some essentials in my backyard, set up a place that would rival Disneyland, and stood in front of my house yelling:

Carnival of Wonders ... 25¢

Neighborhood kids gathered, and we entered the backyard through our tall, red gate into a land of mystery, excitement, and adventure. It was the greatest of my creations and would no doubt change how theme parks and carnivals would operate in the future.

I took my childhood friends (after making sure each paid the 25¢ entrance fee) to a corner of the yard, and we started the first carnival game: throwing a football into a bucket of water. Who was brave and strong enough to accomplish this superhuman feat?

We eventually transitioned to the swing set, where we risked our lives to sore into the open sky. We spent time excavating the sandbox to look for buried treasure. And we climbed into the tall, wooden fort built by my dad to survey the Savannah looking for wild animals (seagulls and the occasional stray dog) in the park behind our house.

• • • • •

Eventually, my desire shifted from earning money to wanting to be the best in anything I did. I am not gifted at sports—though I do love playing ultimate frisbee and disc golf—so rather than athletics, I threw myself into academics, leadership clubs, the church youth group, and my job at a Christian bookstore.

I strove to get the best grades, the right recommendations, and a resume that would wow any college or future employer. When I began college, I got involved in business opportunities, leadership conferences, and anything else that would get me ahead of the crowd.

But a year after college, I began to realize that my efforts were proving futile. I grew up in church and seemed to know the right answers and facts about the Bible, but during a summer internship with an evangelist named Stephen Manley, Jesus began to turn my world on its head.

I had always wanted to be the best, to have the greatest opportunities available, and to make something of myself. But Jesus was calling me to lay it all aside and embrace Him.

And so I did—and nothing has been the same since.

Rather than attempting to be the best, I surrendered to the King of kings and Lord of lords. Rather than running my own life and making a name for myself, I embraced humility and turned my life over to Jesus—to the One who wanted authority and access to do whatever He pleased in and through my life.

I gave it all up ... and found that I had gained far more in Jesus than I ever relinquished.

And it was during this summer internship with Stephen Manley that I discovered a Scripture passage about the Apostle Paul that radically changed my life—and continues to do so.

The Best of the Best

In his letter to the Philippians, Paul exhorts the believers to have a life of unity, holiness, and unwavering joy—a reality that is only possible in Christ Jesus.

As he moves into chapter three, Paul makes a fascinating statement. He looks back on his life and describes the confidence he once had in the flesh (his own self-effort and selfishness). He says, "If anyone else thinks he may have confidence in the flesh, I more so." In other words, if anyone else thinks he's a big shot, if someone thinks he has something to brag about—he has nothing on me. Paul then begins to list his resume, declaring how he is the "best of the best":

If anyone else thinks he may have confidence in the flesh, I more so: circumcised the eighth day, of the stock of Israel, of the tribe of Benjamin, a Hebrew of the Hebrews; concerning the law, a Pharisee; concerning zeal, persecuting the church; concerning the righteousness which is in the law, blameless. But what things were gain to me, these I have counted loss for Christ. Yet indeed I also count all things loss for the excellence of the knowledge of Christ Jesus my Lord, for whom I have suffered the loss of all things, and count them as rubbish, that I may gain Christ and be found in Him, not having my own righteousness, which is from the law, but that which is through faith in Christ, the righteousness which is from God by faith; that I may know Him and the power of His resurrection, and the fellowship of His sufferings, being conformed to His death, if, by any means, I may attain to the resurrection from the dead. Not that I have already attained, or am already perfected; but I press on, that I may lay hold of that for which Christ Jesus has also laid hold of me (Philippians 3.4b–12).

Though it may not appear very impressive in today's culture, in verses five and six Paul gives what would be the "Michael Jordan" or "Bill Gates" statement of success for a Jewish man in the first century—Paul was:

- **circumcised on the eighth day** — taking the symbol of God's covenant upon his flesh, and doing so on the day that God prescribed
- **an Israelite** — not a proselyte Gentile who converted, but a native Israelite—born into the people chosen by God
- **from the tribe of Benjamin** — the tribe that adhered to Judah when all other tribes revolted
- **a Hebrew of Hebrews** — an Israelite on both sides of the family—none of his ancestors had mixed with Gentiles, and he was therefore a "pure-blooded Jew"
- **a Pharisee** — trained at the highest levels concerning the Law, sitting under the teaching of Gamaliel (a prominent scholar of the Law). He was not only a Pharisee, but the son of a Pharisee (see Acts 23.6), and he lived according to the strictest sect of the Jewish religion (see Acts 26.5)
- **a persecutor of the church** — not merely a religious observer, but an active participant—one who not only made a strict profession of faith, but zealously hunted down and persecuted those who were seen as enemies to Jewish belief (i.e., Christians)

- **considered blameless according to the righteousness of the Law** — Paul lived above reproach in every observance to the Law; he lived according to the letter of the Law and fulfilled all outward requirements of it

Perhaps you don't lean back in your chair and whisper a soft "wow" under your breath, but Paul's accomplishments were something to note in his day. Few could claim to have lived according to such high standards.

Yet, looking back upon his life, Paul makes a bold and rather startling statement when he says:

But what things were gain to me, these I have counted loss for Christ. Yet indeed I also count all things loss for the excellence of the knowledge of Christ Jesus my Lord, for whom I have suffered the loss of all things, and count them as rubbish, that I may gain Christ and be found in Him ... (Philippians 3.7-9a).

Paul looks back upon his accolades and achievements and declares them to be "rubbish" in light of knowing Christ Jesus.

Rubbish? What an interesting (and slightly disturbing) word choice.

Dog Dung

Rubbish.

The word conjures up mental images of overflowing trash cans and day-old diapers, moldy banana peels and memories of my brother's dirty socks.

Rubbish—not something I want my hands to touch, much less want to drag into my house. But when you look at the word in its original language, it paints an even more disturbing picture.

Rubbish. It's the Greek word

σκύβαλον | skybalon

Skybalon is not just "rubbish" as you would think of trash—it conveys the idea of refuse. The literal definition is "dog dung"—any refuse, as the excrement of animals, offscourings, rubbish, dregs; of things worthless and detestable.

You're right: gross.

Paul looked back upon his life and counted it as "rubbish" in light of Christ Jesus. It's not that his life was a waste, but when he compared his accomplishments, abilities, wisdom, background, education, and everything else to Jesus, he found (much like we do) that it didn't amount to much—in fact, it was little more than dog dung.

He says, in essence, that if you were to take all of his "best of the best" (his pedigree, education, training, accomplishments, abilities, etc.) and pile them into one heap, he would look and call it "rubbish" in view of knowing Christ Jesus his Lord.

To fully comprehend the weight of what Paul is saying, we must look at what he means by "knowing" Jesus.

Knowing Jesus

It has been said that English is a thin language. Though certain words do carry a depth of meaning, much of our language is surface-level and can have a variety of interpretations.

For example, we use the word "love" to express different things:

- I love ice cream
- I love my wife
- I love my car
- I love my dog
- I love God

I assume we don't mean that we love ice cream on the same level as we love our spouse or that my affection for my vehicle ranks on the same level as my love for God ... right?

We have one word for "love," and we use it to describe a multitude of things. The Greeks, however, had four different words for "love" that they could use when describing distinct concepts. Greek was a "thick language" complex enough to express a deep concept or meaning.

I was once told that the Greeks loved to debate philosophy on their street corners—but one reason this was so popular was because they had a language that was able to handle philosophical depths.

In the Greek, there are predominantly three words that are translated "to know." Each of these three words give a different emphasis in meaning and is important in order to understand our passage in Philippians 3.

So that we can fully understand what Paul means by "knowing Jesus," let's take a few moments to look at each of these Greek words.

1. Gnostos

Gnostos has a focus on facts, data, and information. We get the English word "gnostic" from this word, which described those who placed such an importance on knowledge that they shunned everything else, including the physical word.

Gnostos knowledge isn't bad. In fact, every time you sit down to answer a math question you are engaging in gnostos. A couple examples of gnostos would be:

- 2+2=4
- Picking up a piece of newspaper and reading that the Queen of England has tea every day at promptly 4:00 p.m.

Science, math, newspapers. Gnostos. Data, facts, information.

This words shows up several times in Scripture, one place being Acts 1.19.

Jesus had recently risen from the dead and forty days later ascended into heaven. The disciples have gathered in the upper room for the first official business meeting of the early church.

Peter stands up in their midst and, talking about Judas Iscariot who betrayed Jesus, declares:

> *"Men and brethren, this Scripture had to be fulfilled, which the Holy Spirit spoke before by the mouth of David concerning Judas, who became a guide to those who arrested Jesus; for he was numbered with us and obtained a part in this ministry." (Now this man purchased a field with the wages of iniquity; and falling headlong, he burst open in the middle and all his entrails gushed out. And it became **known** to all those dwelling in Jerusalem; so that field is called in their own language, Akel Dama, that is, Field of Blood)* (Acts 1.16–19).

In the middle of Peter's statement, Luke (the writer of Acts) makes a parenthetical statement to give clarity to the event involving Judas. Luke says that a field was purchased and that Judas killed himself there, which was known by everyone who dwelt in Jerusalem.

How did everyone in Jerusalem know about the death of Judas? Did everyone know him personally and then realize what had happened after he didn't show up for a meeting? Obviously not. How did they know? Well, that morning they stepped outside and grabbed their *Jerusalem Times*, and on the front page it read, "Man Died. Entrails Gushed Out. Field Now Called Field of Blood."

They didn't know Judas personally, yet they all heard about his death—but it wasn't anything more to them than facts, data, and information. Newspaper kind of stuff.

Gnostos.

2. Oida

Whereas gnostos focuses on facts, data, and information, oida is about perception. It has the idea of "to see"—not with the eyes, but with the mind.

You are told something, and you respond with, "Oh, I see!" It's not that you "see" it, but you "see" it ... see what I mean? In other words, you don't physically see it, but you perceive, understand, and grasp what they are telling you. The lightbulb has turned on!

In John 13-17, Jesus and His disciples have gathered together to celebrate the Feast of the Passover. Jesus washes their feet in chapter 13 and then enters a discussion with them that lasts several chapters. In John 14, Jesus tells them that He is going to prepare a place for them. Thomas speaks up and says, "Lord, we do not **know** where You are going, and how can we **know** the way?" This is the word oida. Thomas is saying, "Jesus we do not oida where you are going—we do not see, we don't perceive, we have no idea where You are going—how can we oida the way?" Jesus looks at him, no doubt thinking, "Thomas, buddy, you've been with me for three years ..." and makes His famous statement:

I am the way, the truth, and the life. No one comes to the Father except through Me (John 14.6).

Oida—perception and understanding.

3. Ginosko

This is easily one of my all-time favorite Greek words. Ginosko isn't focused so much upon facts, data, and information or upon perception and understanding—ginosko is knowing something through experience or relationship.

This word has a variety of uses throughout the Bible, one of which is the kind of intimacy (knowing) a husband and wife share. For example, the angel Gabriel appears to Mary and tells her that she will become pregnant. Mary responds to Gabriel by asking, "How can this be, since I do not *know* a man?" (Luke 1.34).

Obviously Mary is not asking, "What is a man? Can you point one out to me?" What she is saying is, "I have never been with a man sexually—so how can I be pregnant?" This word "know" is the Greek word ginosko.

This same idea appears again when Gabriel goes to Joseph to tell him that Mary is with child. In Matthew 1.24–25 we read, "Then Joseph, being awakened from sleep, did as the angel of the Lord commanded him and took to him his wife, and did not *know* her till she had brought forth her firstborn Son. And he called His name JESUS."

Biblically, this word doesn't just refer to marital intimacy between a husband and a wife, it also refers to knowledge acquired through experience. Let me give you a couple examples:

Some time ago I was driving and noticed a sign that read "Speed Limit 45." If you asked me what the speed limit was on that road, I would have quickly told you 45 miles per hour—but that is gnostos kind of knowing: facts, data, information. While driving on the same road a few days later, I noticed in my rearview mirror a car with flashing blue, red, and white lights. I decided to pull over to the side of the road, and the car behind me did likewise. A man in a blue uniform walked up to my window and asked for my license and registration, which I kindly (and quickly) gave him. He handed me a small slip of paper commemorating our time together on the side of the road, and I was forced to pay a fee of $200 as a way to say thanks. If you were to ask me then what the speed limit was on that road, I would have told you 45 miles per hour —not because I saw the sign, but because I *experienced* the speed limit (or in reality the penalty of breaking it).

To give another illustration, several months ago I was interested in a particular topic. I'm not married (yet), but I was fascinated to know more about kissing. What was I to do? Well, I did what any red-blooded, American male would do ... I got on Wikipedia and looked it up. I read all the details —the different types of kissing, the technique of how to kiss and breathe correctly—I looked at the charts and graphs, and I even saw a painting of Romeo and Juliet. I learned all about kissing.

If I shared this with you in person, I imagine you would look at me funny ... because while this *is* one way to know (gnostos) about kissing, there is a better way—through experience (ginosko).

The Cute Old Couple

The big day has finally arrived. The wedding party is at the altar, the vows are given, the kiss is memorable, and as you walk to the back to shake his hand, you ask the groom, "Do you know your wife?"

"Yes!" he beams. "She is 5'8", has blonde hair and green eyes, and likes long walks on the beach."

"No, no," you reply. "Do you *know* her?"

"Well ... yeah. I know what she likes and what gets her excited about life. I know what causes her face to brighten, and I have seen what she's like when tragedy hits. Yes, I know her because I have spent time with her."

Ginosko is all about knowing something through experience and relationship. This isn't information you read about in a book—this is knowledge you gain because you went through something, because you were involved, because of experience or relationship.

Have you ever seen a cute old couple? I love cute old couples. In fact, I can't wait till I become a cute old couple (though that brings a need to be married first). Have you ever been around a couple who has been married for over fifty years? Oftentimes a couple who has spent that much time together knows each other so well that they have their own unique language. They use words, phrases, and facial expressions that communicate to each other in ways that others can't understand. In fact, they may not even have to talk at all—they just know what each other is thinking. Couples who have fifty years of life experience and relationship together often know each other so well that they talk like each other, act like each other, and even start to look like each other. That is a ginosko type of knowing.

Eternal Life

The word "ginosko" shows up all throughout the New Testament, but one powerful example is found in the High Priestly Prayer of John 17. While praying, Jesus says in verse three, "This is eternal life ..."

Have you ever wanted to know what eternal life is? Have you ever been interested in discovering its secret? Jesus tells us exactly what eternal life is:

> *This is eternal life, that they may <u>know</u> You, the only true God, and Jesus Christ whom You have sent (John 17.3).*

The word for "know" in this passage is ginosko. Eternal life is not knowing facts and details about God; it isn't going to church, reading your Bible, praying, or even tithing (though these are all good things). What determines if you make it to heaven is not passing a true/false test, being a member of the correct denomination, or having a bunch of head knowledge about the Word of God. Eternal life is *knowing* Jesus—actually knowing Him—getting wrapped up in relationship and intimacy with the God of the universe.

Having relationship and oneness with Jesus is like becoming a cute old couple with Him. It's knowing Him (ginosko) to the point where I start to talk like Him, think like Him, and act like Him—not because I'm trying to imitate His life but because I'm wrapped up in intimacy with Him—as He, through the Holy Spirit, indwells my life.

Ginosko: knowing that moves beyond mere academics and into the realm of relationship.

I want deliberately to encourage this mighty longing after God. The lack of it has brought us to our present low estate. The stiff and wooden quality about our religious lives is a result of our lack of holy desire. Complacency is a deadly foe of all spiritual growth. Acute desire must be present or there will be no manifestation of Christ to His people. He waits to be wanted. Too bad that with many of us He waits so long, so very long, in vain.

– AW Tozer –

Philippians 3

Now let's (finally) take our understanding of these Greek words and return to Philippians 3.

Yet indeed I also count all things loss for the excellence of the knowledge of Christ Jesus my Lord, for whom I have suffered the loss of all things, and count them as rubbish, that I may gain Christ ... (Philippians 3.8).

Again, Paul is talking about being the "best of the best." He says if you were to take his education, background, family, wisdom, talents, abilities, awards, trophies, and all else, compile them, and lay the heap before him, he would look at it and call it rubbish (dog dung) in view of **knowing** Jesus.

This leads to the question: Which word for "knowing" does Paul use in the passage?

When I first came to this section, I assumed Paul used the word *ginosko*. Obviously he is saying that he is willing to exchange everything for an intimate relationship with Jesus ... right? But surprisingly, that's not the word he uses.

The Newspaper Headline

Yet indeed I also count all things loss for the excellence of the <u>knowledge</u> of Christ Jesus my Lord ... (Philippians 3.8).

Paul uses the word *gnostos*—facts, data, information.

Doesn't that seem odd to you?

Paul writes that he is willing to give up everything—to count all things as rubbish—in order to simply know Jesus on the same level as picking up a newspaper and reading a headline that says "Jesus is Lord." No relationship. No intimacy. Just facts, data, information, 2+2=4, newspaper headlines.

There is an amazing nugget of truth contained in this. Do you realize how incredible, how phenomenal, how _____ (insert your favorite superlative here) Jesus is? Our Jesus is so magnificent, extraordinary, and impressive that He is worth giving up everything for—even if we never had the ability to have a relationship with Him. He is worthy of all praise, glory, and adoration—even if I never got to experience daily intimacy with Him. He deserves my "everything"—

even if all I ever had access to was a single newspaper headline that read "Jesus is Lord." This single newspaper clipping is worth calling my entire life rubbish.

Wanting So Much More

"However," Paul declares, "I will not be satisfied by a mere newspaper version of knowing Jesus. I want to know (ginosko) Him!"

In verse eight Paul says he would willingly call his life "rubbish" in view of knowing (gnostos) Christ Jesus his Lord—he would exchange everything in his life for having a single newspaper headline about Him. But Paul goes on in verse ten to cry out that his passion, desire, focus, and consumption is this:

> ... that I may **know** Him and the power of His resurrection, and the fellowship of His sufferings, being conformed to His death, if, by any means, I may attain to the resurrection from the dead (Philippians 3.10–11).

The word "know" in verse ten is ginosko—knowing Jesus through relationship and intimacy—the same kind of knowing that Jesus uses to talk about eternal life in John 17.3.

Paul says he would exchange everything for knowing *about* Jesus, but his one goal, his single aim, the one beat of his heart is to actually **know** Jesus—not just facts and information *about* Him, but intimacy and relationship **with** Him.

Knowing vs Intimacy

The Seminary Cemetery

There has long been a joke that those who attend seminary for Bible training are often the deadest people in the church.

In 2005, I found myself at seminary, which ironically was next door to a large cemetery. Before leaving home and heading halfway across the country to study for my M.Div. degree, my aunt pulled me aside and cautioned me not to lose my faith while in school. I don't remember my response, but I imagine it involved a fit of laughter and a bit of scoffing. Lose my faith? Did she know where I was going? I was heading to a school where I assumed we would study the Bible for homework, spend hours talking about Jesus in and out of class, and sing Kumbayah around a campfire at night.

When I arrived, I was excited—surely these people would be the most on-fire Christians in the world. Yet what I found saddened me. While there were many at my school who genuinely loved

Jesus and sought after Him, there were countless others who knew a lot *about* Jesus but didn't actually *know* Him. And there is a radical difference.

I would sit in class and see people who grew up in church, had all the stories memorized, knew big theological lingo, and could debate you up and down, yet they lacked substance, intimacy, and life. They had a form of godliness, but it was wrapped up in information, dissertations, debate, and data.

What they failed to realize is that information doesn't save you; knowing all the facts and data doesn't get you to heaven. Even having the entire Bible memorized doesn't give you a leg up in the eternal life department.

Don't get me wrong—I'm a huge proponent of studying the Bible; I love to read the Word and desire to memorize big portions of it. Yet while these are all good things, they don't save me. Jesus saves me. Again, John 17.3 declares, "This is eternal life, that they may **know** You, the only true God, and Jesus Christ whom You have sent"—not knowing information about Him, but actually knowing Him.

Demonic Knowledge

Do you know that the demons know Jesus? They likely spied on His activity when He walked upon the earth, they were involved in encounters with Him several times, and, during the wilderness temptation, Satan is seen having parts of the Bible memorized. Yet though they may know a lot about Jesus (facts, data, information), they don't intimately and relationally know Him (ginosko).

If all we have is facts, data, and information about Jesus, we don't have anything better than the demons (and if you didn't already know, the demons don't get to experience eternity in heaven).

"But I've said the sinner's prayer!" you retort.

Good for you. But what passes off as the "sinner's prayer" today is often little more than a true/false test—a test even the demons could pass.

1. Do you believe Jesus came to earth as a man? ... **True**

2. Do you believe Jesus died upon the Cross? ... **True**

3. Do you believe Jesus rose again three days later? ... **True**

Congratulations, brother! You're now a Christian!

But that is not how you find eternal life. Eternal life is found in a Person: Jesus. The key to salvation is a relationship. What determines whether you go to heaven or to hell is not if you have enough facts about the Bible, grew up in the right church, came from the right parents, have the proper creeds memorized, or can do verbal gymnastics and use the right phraseology. What determines your eternal destination is whether or not you intimately know (ginosko) Jesus.

The Mouse and the Cookie Jar

I once heard a humorous story about a mouse who crawled up onto a kitchen counter and discovered a cookie jar. To the delight of the little mouse, there was a spoon lying nearby that she could lean against the jar to scamper to its top. The jar happened to be open, and as the little mouse reached the top, she stumbled and fell into the jar. The moment she hit the mound of cookies, she cried out with unspeakable joy, "I'm a cookie!"

Would you agree with her? Of course not. The little mouse doesn't become a cookie merely because she found herself inside a cookie jar—and it is just as ridiculous to think that you are a Christian merely because you have stumbled into a church building. Attending church on Sundays, no matter how religiously, doesn't make you a Christian—only knowing (ginosko-ing) Jesus makes you a Christian.

"I'm not sure I'm a Christian," you say. "How will I know?"

Simple. Do you know Jesus? I didn't ask if you know information about Him, if you read your Bible, or if you spend hours upon your knees—the question is this: Do you *know* Him? Are you wrapped up in intimacy and oneness with Jesus Christ?

Man was so engineered by God that the presence of the Creator within the creature is indispensable to his humanity.

– Ian Thomas –

The moment you come to realize that only God can make a man godly, you are left with no option but to find God, and to know God, and to let God be God in and through you.

– Ian Thomas –

Living a Ginosko Life

Knowing Jesus

I have long had the desire to know Jesus intimately. I don't want a casual friendship with Jesus, I want an ever-increasing relationship with Him.

One of the aspects of *ginosko* that I love is that it never wanes or diminishes; rather, it grows, expands, and becomes richer over time.

I want to know Jesus better today than I knew Him yesterday. I want to know Him better tomorrow than I do today. I want to be more excited and passionate about Jesus and be more intimate with Him next week than I am now, and I want to experience greater riches in Christ next year than I have in the last five combined.

Over the past several years I have prayed that God would so fill me with Himself that when someone met me and came back a year later, he would completely forget my name but remember me as the guy who was filled with the life of Jesus. I don't merely want to imitate Him, I want Him to produce His life in and through me. As I get wrapped up in knowing Him in greater measures, I want my relationship with Jesus to be like the cute old couple who spends so much time together that they both begin to talk, act, and even look the same.

Can you imagine having that with Jesus? A relationship that increases and becomes more rich and fulfilling the longer you live with Him. A relationship where I begin to have His heart, mind, eyes, and attitude. A relationship where I start to act like Him and where the words that come out of my mouth are His words—not because I'm emulating, but because I can't help myself: I'm wrapped up in relationship with Jesus!

I want people to see Jesus—not me—when they look at my life.

Seeing Jesus in My Life

I once heard a story of the great "Prince of Preachers," Charles Spurgeon (1834–1892). This man was madly in love with Jesus and knew Him intimately (ginosko). One day, Spurgeon was going to preach in a town he had never been to before.

As he walked through town, someone saw him and fell to his knees, repenting of his sins.

What did Spurgeon have that compelled someone to be confronted with his sins and cry out in repentance? Could it have been that Spurgeon knew Jesus so well that when people saw him, they didn't see Spurgeon so much as the God who lived inside Him? Is it possible that Jesus can be the focus, the delight, and the desire of our lives so that when we meet people they lose sight of us and only see Christ?

A similar story is told of Henry Clay Morrison (1857–1942). Morrison was working in the corn fields one day when a Methodist circuit rider came by on his horse. Morrison had seen the preacher before and knew he was a holy man. As the preacher passed by, a conviction of sin overtook Morrison, causing him to fall upon his knees and surrender his life to God.

A friend of mine, having heard the story about Morrison's surrender, wrote, "As I pondered this, I couldn't help but cry, 'O God, make me a holy man! Create in me a disdain for sin and a love for holiness so that even sinners take note.' "

Could this be true in our lives? Could we become so wrapped up in intimacy and oneness with our precious Jesus that the people around us see Him in and through our lives?

Father, make me a crisis man.

Bring those I contact to decision.

Let me be a milepost on a single road;

make me a fork, that men must turn one

way or another on facing Christ in me.

– Jim Eillot –

The T-Shirt Temptation

Have you seen the Christian T-shirts available today? Growing up I thought it was the coolest thing to wear Christian T-shirts, and I had a closet full of them. Most of the time they are cheesy knockoffs from pop culture. Let me show you a few.

JOHN THREE
SIXTEEN

Jesus
SWEET SAVIOR
KING OF KINGS

LIFEGUARD

MATTHEW 14:22-32

MINE WALKS ON WATER

Hii Saved Me
John 3:16

Amazing
Grace

HISWAY

Though I have largely forsworn the Christian T-shirt movement, preferring not to use my clothing as a marketing campaign, I did come across a Christian T-shirt several years back that I had to buy. It was just too good to not pick up.

What if the secret to Christianity is **not** found in wearing Christian T-shirts? Wearing them is not bad, but isn't the primary reason we clothe ourselves with such attire to tell the world that we are believers?

What if the world knew we were Christians not by the clothing we wear or the big family Bible we tote under our arm—what if they knew we were Christians because they saw Christ in us?

I wholeheartedly believe that we should share our faith—we should proclaim it from the mountaintops and street corners—but I don't want the primary reason that people know I'm a believer to be because they saw it on my shirt ... I want them to see Jesus in my life!

How is this possible?

It is only found in knowing Him.

Mistaken

Several years ago, a song came out by Warren Barfield that articulates this truth well. Barfield sings:

(Verse 1)

I shouldn't have to tell you who I am
'Cause who I am should be speaking for itself
'Cause if I am who I, I want to be
Then who you see won't even be me
Oh the more and more I disappear
The more He becomes clear

(Chorus)

Till everyone I talk to hears His voice
And everyone I touch feels

the warmth of His hand
Till everyone I meet
Sees Jesus in me
This is all I wanna be
I want to be mistaken for Jesus

(Bridge)
May He touch with my hands
See through my eyes
May He speak through my lips
Live through my life

I, too, want my life to be mistaken for Jesus. I don't become Jesus in a literal sense—but as His Spirit lives and works within me, I decrease, and He increases. I get out of the way, and Jesus becomes the focus. The more I get to know (ginosko) Him, the more I realize that He wants to be the center of my life, and I find myself having His heart, mind, attitude, focus, character, and life.

Christianity isn't about living *for* Christ (in my own self effort), Christianity is about allowing Jesus to live His life through me. And this is one of the tremendous realities of the New Testament: the outside God has come inside!

THE OUTSIDE GOD GETTING INSIDE

In the Old Testament the emphasis was that God was "out there" somewhere looking down upon us. The popular song from the early '90s sums it up well: "God is watching us. God is watching us. God is watching us from a distance."

And while it is true that God is everywhere and does "watch us," the reality is that when you enter into the New Testament, you discover that God has moved from somewhere "out there" to "inside."

The scene in Acts 2 is startling. The disciples were in the upper room, when suddenly their world was turned upside down. The God of the universe came and inhabited their lives. The Spirit, whom Jesus referred to as the "promise of the Father," had come to live within them. It was no longer going to be them working *for* God—now they were going to allow God to work *through* them. A radical shift had taken place (which continues to this day): the outside God had come to dwell inside!

What an amazing and exciting reality!

No longer am I to pull off the Christian life in my own strength, resource, and ability (like people were commanded in the Old Testament—where righteousness, holiness, and godliness was left mainly to their ability). NOW the outside God has come inside my life and wants to live His life through mine!

The Impossible Christian Life

The fact is, the Christian life is impossible to live. The standards are too high, the demands are too great, and the constant victory required is too much for my own ability and wisdom. I can't pull it off!

This is one of the facts that the Old Testament reveals. Under the Law, it was impossible to live a righteous, holy, good, and godly life in one's own strength and ability. Isaiah 64.6 says that even our best deeds are like filthy rags.

When you come to the New Testament, Jesus takes the standards of the Old Covenant and elevates them—He makes them even harder. In the Old you couldn't murder; in the New you can't even hate. In the Old you couldn't commit adultery, even though you thought about doing it; in the New, lust was even forbidden. Over and over, Jesus elevated the standards of the Law (see Matthew 5, for example).

If it was impossible to be holy and righteous in the Old Testament, how much harder is it to live godly in the New? The impossible was made even more impossible.

But a solution was given—the infilling of the Holy Spirit.

We are to be perfect as our Father in heaven is perfect, not by struggle and effort, but by the impartation of that which is perfect.

– Oswald Chambers –

The Secret to Success in Christianity

Jesus told His disciples to wait for the infilling of His Spirit. And when the Spirit entered the disciples at Pentecost, the impossible suddenly became possible.

As you follow their story throughout the book of Acts, one thing becomes evident—their lives could only be explained in terms of Jesus. Over and over again, the leaders and rulers of the day were surprised and marveled to find that the disciples were "untrained and uneducated" men.

The book of Acts has often been called the "Acts of the Apostles," but that misses the emphasis of the entire book. It wasn't the acts of the apostles, it was the "Acts of the Holy Spirit" in and through the apostles.

They surrendered themselves to the working of the Holy Spirit in their lives, and Jesus Christ demonstrated Himself to the world through the Holy Spirit—so much so that the disciples were accused of "turning the world upside down" (Acts 17.6).

The secret to success in Christianity is to stop attempting to live out Christianity in your own strength and resource—instead, live fully surrendered to and dependent upon the Spirit of God in your life. Rather than strive, try, struggle, and attempt to do the impossible on your own, allow the Holy Spirit to produce His life, His ministry, and His character within you.

The outside God has come inside!

Your religious life is every day to be a proof that God works impossibilities; your religious life is to be a series of impossibilities made possible and actual by God's almighty power.

– Andrew Murray –

The greatness of a man's power is the measure of his surrender.

– William Booth –

Lackadaisical Living and a Change of Source

Let me clarify that I am not promoting laziness. The Christian life is not one where you sink down on a couch, eat bonbons, and wait for God to push you off and force you to do something. The Christian life is an interaction between the Living God and the believer—it is a change of source.

Up to this point most of us have attempted to produce the Christian life in our strength, wisdom, and ability. We strive, struggle, and attempt to live this impossible life apart from God. What I'm emphasizing is neither "I'll do it myself" nor "I won't do anything until God forces me to"—this is about allowing the Spirit of God to have authority and sway in my life. I'm not living my life *for* Christ, I'm interacting with God as we (together) live out each day.

In a healthy marriage, each spouse doesn't give fifty percent to the relationship, they both give one hundred. Likewise, in the Christian life, I don't give ninety percent while God chips in the other ten, and neither does God give ninety percent and leave the other ten to me. We both interact together in relationship, each giving one hundred percent.

The Christian life is about a change of source. No longer do I live out of my ability and resource; rather, I lean on, depend upon, and surrender myself to the ability and resource that God wants to demonstrate in my life through the Spirit. I trust Jesus Christ, the Faithful One, to guide my life, give me wisdom beyond my own intellect, and pull off the impossible life that I've never been able to live on my own.

The Only Explanation For Your Life

Major Ian Thomas wrote in his book *The Mystery of Godliness*:

> The Christian life can be explained only in terms of Jesus Christ, and if your life as a Christian can still be explained in terms of you—your personality, your willpower, your gift, your talent, your money, your courage, your scholarship, your dedication, your sacrifice, or your anything—then although you may have the Christian life, you are not yet living it! If the way you live your life as a Christian can be explained in terms of you, what have you to offer to the man who

lives next door? The way he lives his life can be explained in terms of him, and so far as he is concerned, you happen to be "religious"—but he is not! "Christianity" may be your hobby, but it is not his, and there is nothing about the way you practice it which strikes him as at all remarkable! There is nothing about you which leaves him guessing, and nothing commendable of which he does not feel himself equally capable without the inconvenience of becoming a Christian! ... It has got to become obvious to others that the kind of life you are living is ... beyond all human explanation! That it is beyond the consequences of man's capacity to imitate, and however little they may understand this, it is clearly the consequence only of God's capacity to reproduce Himself in you!

When people look at your life, can they explain how you live in terms of YOU? Do people look at your life and think, "Yeah, I could live that way if I wanted"? Or when they look at your life, does it leave them guessing—unsure how it's possible to live in such a way?

I long to have a life that is beyond all human explanation. I don't merely want to imitate the life of Christ, I want to know Him on such a deep, personal, and intimate level—indwelt by His Spirit —so that it is not I who live but Christ who lives within me and so that the life I now live, I live by faith in the Son of God, who loved me and gave Himself for me (Galatians 2.20).

The impossible life *is* possible to live!—but not in your own strength, resource, and ability. It is only the Person of Jesus indwelling your life through His Spirit that allows you to live in a way that is impossible in the natural realm.

And when the world sees you live an impossible life—when they see you living in daily victory, bearing the fruit of the Spirit abundantly (see Galatians 5.22–23), and increasing in the wisdom, character, attitude, and nature of Jesus—it becomes an incredible testimony of God's goodness, grace, grandeur, and glory. For the only explanation of your life becomes Jesus Christ.

Jesus Christ does not want to be our helper; He wants to be our life. He does not want us to work for Him; He wants us to let Him do His work through us, using us as we use a pencil to write with—better still, using us as one of the fingers on His hand.

– Charles Trumbull –

Do You Know Jesus?

The Christian life is all about intimacy with the Most High God. The prophets of old talked about it and yearned to have it. The disciples experienced the fullness of this reality at Pentecost, and it is now available for you and me to embrace in daily, moment-by-moment living.

The intimacy and oneness we are talking about is not a mere factual knowing. This is not about how much information you can gather in Sunday school, how many stories you can memorize, how many verses you can quote, or whether or not you went to Bible college. This is about having relationship with Jesus Christ—a vibrant intimacy and oneness that continues to grow, deepen, and become richer and more life-transforming as time goes on.

It's great that you go to church, spend time in prayer and Bible study, and read the articles and musings on deeperChristian.com (bonus points for this last one)—but in the end, it is all for naught if you don't have Jesus.

Once again, John 17.3 declares, "And this is eternal life, that they may *know* You, the only true God, and Jesus Christ whom You have sent."

Ginosko. A knowledge not based on facts, data, and information, but upon relationship and experience.

Cry out with Paul that your passion, desire, and focus is that you "may know Him and the power of His resurrection, and the fellowship of His sufferings, being conformed to His death ..." (Philippians 3.10).

Yes, Jesus is worth knowing as facts, data, and information. You should memorize Scripture, you should read the Bible often, you should know the stories—and like Paul, having a single newspaper headline that reads "Jesus is Lord" is worth calling everything in your life "rubbish" in comparison. But may we not be satisfied with mere content, stories, and data. Let us embrace the King of kings and Lord of lords in relationship and oneness.

Ginosko. A knowledge that grows and continually increases and expands as time goes on.

The level of intimacy I have with Jesus should be greater next year than it is right now. Day by day I should grow in surrender and dependency, relationship and intimacy, as I continually abide in Him.

Oh, to know Jesus, walk in His Holy Spirit, and be the vessel through which He lives and demonstrates His life!

The mark of a life governed by the Holy Spirit is that such a life is continually and ever more and more occupied with Christ, that Christ is becoming greater and greater as time goes on. ... Oh, the depths, the fullness, of Christ! If we live as long as ever man lived, we shall still be only on the fringe of this vast fullness that Christ is.

– T. Austin-Sparks –

Christ is either Lord of all,
or He is not Lord at all.

– Hudson Taylor –

Having made Jesus your all, you shall find
all in Jesus.

– Charles Spurgeon –

Trying to do the Lord's work in your own
strength is the most confusing, exhausting,
and tedious of all work. But when you are
filled with the Holy Spirit, then the ministry
of Jesus just flows out of you.

– Corrie ten Boom –

Apart from Me you can do nothing!

– Jesus –

Appendix

5 Simple Ways to Take Your Relationship with Jesus to the Next Level

---

For direct links to each of the following resources, please visit **deeperChristian.com/knowingJesus**

---

1. Spend time with Jesus

As the cliché states, it's not so much about quantity of time as it is about quality of time. But in your relationship with Jesus, you *can* have quality AND constant intimacy with Jesus since He lives inside you. It is possible to "pray without ceasing" as Paul commands in 1 Thessalonians 5.17. Learn more about this incredible reality in the deeperChristian article *The Need to Cultivate Daily Intimacy with Jesus.*

2. Learn how to "saturate" in His Word

Studying the Bible is more than punching a time clock—it is all about knowing Jesus and soaking in His Truth, allowing the author to reveal Himself to you. Saturation Bible Study goes beyond the normal academic study and purposely goes after Jesus to know (ginosko) Him intimately. This is one of the most central things in my life and has born a decade of growth and depth in me. Start learning what it means to saturate in God's Word with this helpful overview entitled *How to Study the Bible.*

3. Become Obsessed

This entire book has talked about being obsessed with Jesus and increasing in love and passion for Him day by day. Many of us forget that we are created to be obsessed, and in truth, we all have something in our lives that we "obsess" over —shouldn't that be Jesus? I recommend that you listen to Dr. Stephen Manley's sermon *Obsessed*, which gives a handful of illustrations depicting how we are obsessed and what it means to be obsessed with Jesus.

4. Read good books

Reading Christian classics is a great addition to a believer's life. Books like those listed below encourage your faith, challenge your soul, and press you into Jesus as they give you rich food for thought. You can download my **recommended reading list**, but the following books deal with a similar theme as this book:

- **Absolute Surrender** – Andrew Murray
- **The Mystery of Godliness** – Major Ian Thomas
- **God's Pursuit of Man** – A.W. Tozer
- **The Pursuit of God** – A.W. Tozer
- **How to Live the Victorious Christian Life** – Unknown Christian
- **Abide in Christ** – Andrew Murray
- **Victory in Christ** – Charles Trumbull
- **Humility** – Andrew Murray
- **Practicing the Presence of God** – Brother Lawrence
- **Being What You've Become** – Stephen Manley
- **God's Missionary** – Amy Carmichael
- **Why Revival Tarries** – Leonard Ravenhill
- **Rees Howells: Intercessor** – Norman Grubb
- **C.T. Studd: Cricketer and Pioneer** – Norman Grubb
- **Hudson Taylor's Spiritual Secret** – Dr. and Mrs. Howard Taylor
- **They Found the Secret** – V. Raymond Edman

5. Pour your life out to the world around you

The Christian life isn't meant to be cooped up and hidden from the world. We are meant to pour our lives out for the world around us—just like Jesus did. Jesus was constantly pouring His life out —bleeding, suffering, and dying to serve those around Him. His words not only proclaimed the Gospel, His life showcased it! When you allow Jesus to invade your life through the indwelling Holy Spirit, He will not let you remain the same. He will use your life as a pen in His hand to effect change for His Kingdom and His glory. Want to read more? Check out the article called *The Lifestyle of the Cross.*

Bonus Ideas

This is a bit of self-promotion, but the following two ideas have greatly blessed, challenged, and enriched my life—so I thought I would share them with you.

6. Attend a conference

I love solid, Jesus-focused conferences! There is something about being in an environment with a group of like-minded believers that is encouraging. A conference that is not there for fluff but for the edification of the Christian is rare these days. Over the years I have preached at or been involved with the following conferences, all of which I highly recommend (to learn more about these, please visit: **deeperChristian.com/knowingJesus**).

Cross Style Training Camp & Conference

This was the conference that originally changed my life. Started by evangelist Dr. Stephen Manley, this conference held every June (and a shorter version each January) is a week of intense discipleship, Biblical training, preaching, worship, and fellowship. Special teaching sessions are given each morning to dive into topics like Saturation Bible Study, the life of the believer, and understanding Biblical theology. This conference is free (housing and meals not included) and held not far from Nashville in Lebanon, Tennessee (simulcast options are available as well).

Bravehearted Man Conference [for men only]

The *Bravehearted Man Conference* (and simulcast) was started by Eric Ludy and is hosted yearly at the Ellerslie Campus in Windsor, Colorado. This conference is a weekend designed to stick the grit back in the Christian man, the pluck back in the preacher, the heart back in the father, the purpose back in the husband, and the life back in the believer. This conference pulls no punches and promises no comfort. It is not a retreat, but rather a call to the front lines of war, working to see men made ready in this hour of dire need to live strongly, suffer joyfully, and die triumphantly for the glory of Jesus Christ.

Set-Apart Girl Conference [for women only]

The *Set-Apart Girl Conference* is a life-changing weekend for women of all ages. This conference will refresh and revive your spiritual walk and give you a vision for set-apart femininity that is both beautiful and practical—helping you exchange spiritual mediocrity for passionate devotion to Jesus Christ. This conference is hosted at the Ellerslie campus in Windsor, Colorado, and features the teaching of Leslie Ludy and often several guest speakers. If you cannot attend the conference live, you can watch online via simulcast.

7. Read deeperChristian and subscribe to the daily Quotes

It has been a deeply enriching experience for me to write about the Christian life and curate great Christian quotes on the deeperChristian websites. We have a multitude of ideas regarding where we want to take the website and ministry in the future, and our prayer is that it becomes a blessing, encouragement, and edification to your intimacy and relationship with Jesus.

deeperChristian blog/online magazine:
deeperChristian.com

deeperChristian quotes (daily):
deeperChristianQuotes.com

• • • • •

On a final note, know that the deeperChristian community and I are cheering you ever deeper into the Person of Jesus Christ! May your life be all about Him.

Your friend and fellow companion on the Narrow Way,

NRJohnson

For this reason I bow my knees to the Father of our Lord Jesus Christ, from whom the whole family in heaven and earth is named, that He would grant you, according to the riches of His glory, to be strengthened with might through His Spirit in the inner man, that Christ may dwell in your hearts through faith; that you, being rooted and grounded in love, may be able to comprehend with all the saints what is the width and length and depth and height —to **know** (ginosko) the love of Christ which passes knowledge (gnostos); **that you may be filled with all the fullness of God**. Now to Him who is able to do exceedingly abundantly above all that we ask or think, according to the power that works in us, to Him be glory in the church by Christ Jesus to all generations, forever and ever. Amen.

– Ephesians 3.14–21 –

ABOUT DEEPERCHRISTIAN

Looking at the "Christian" church of today, I am deeply saddened by its current state of affairs: the lack of victory within believers' lives, the diminishment of the authority and truth of God's Word, the plague of worldliness in the church (and believers' lives), Biblical illiteracy, the lack of evangelism, a spiritual stupor, a fear of man, and an acceptance of sin.

We have become much like the group Paul warned Timothy about in 2 Timothy 3.1-5:

But know this, that in the last days perilous times will come: For men will be lovers of themselves, lovers of money, boasters, proud, blasphemers, disobedient to parents, unthankful, unholy, unloving, unforgiving, slanderers, without self-control, brutal, despisers of good, traitors, headstrong, haughty, lovers of pleasure rather than lovers of God, having a form of godliness but denying its power. And from such people turn away!

The need of the Church today is to return to our "first love," Jesus Christ (see Revelation 2.4). A return not in words only, but in heart, mind, soul, and strength. A return to historic Christianity—a Christianity that actually works. A return to a life focused and dependent upon Jesus Christ—filled with His Spirit and enabled to live victorious and godly lives. A return to a full givenness and surrender to the will of God—desiring to be spilled and spent for His renown and glory. We must decrease and get out of the way so that He can increase and be seen.

And yet Christians today are seemingly lost.

- We are told to study the Bible, but we don't know how.

- We know we are supposed to pray, but we're not sure where to start or how to pray for longer than a few minutes.

- We read Scripture and realize that our lives are to be free and victorious, not marred with sin, defeat, and despair.

- Our lives often feel like they are lacking substance, meaning, and power—isn't the Christian's life supposed to turn the world upside down?

- If Jesus has truly changed our lives, shouldn't we want to tell others about it? But we are passive and lifeless, wondering if there's more to this thing called Christianity.

If you have ever felt that way, you're not alone.

Maybe you're looking for answers to the problems listed above; maybe you just want encouragement—in either case, deeperChristian desires to spur you onward and upward in your Christian walk through articles, Bible studies, resources, quotes, book reviews, and media

The end goal of deeperChristian is for you to be more in love with Jesus than ever before, to be filled and sourced by His Spirit, and to know, obey, and be transformed by His Word in increasing measure.

What is the Deeper Christian Life?

Throughout Christian history, the Deeper Christian Life has been called by other names such as: the Exchanged Life, the Victorious Christian Life, the Spirit-Filled (Spirit-Led) Life, or the Narrow Way of the Cross.

Simply put, the Deeper Christian Life is a life focused on, filled with, and dependent upon Jesus Christ. It is a purposeful progression to ever-increasing intimacy and oneness of relationship with the God of the universe. It is being filled with and sourced by the Spirit of God. It is plunging headlong into the endless depths of Jesus, desiring more and more of Him—with the prayer of a kid in a swimming pool of chocolate: "Oh Lord, increase my capacity!"

Through intimacy with Jesus and the power of the indwelling Holy Spirit, Jesus produces and becomes my victory and triumph for everyday living—He is all that I need (see 2 Peter 1.3). As Handley Moule once declared:

> *[The Christian life is] to be like [Christ]. To displace self from the inner throne and to enthrone Him; to make not the slightest compromise with the smallest sin. We aim at nothing less than to walk with God all day long, to abide every hour in Christ, and He and His words in us, to love God with all the heart, and our neighbor as ourselves. . . .*

The Christian life is not focused upon my effort, ability, or duty. It is a singular focus upon the Person of Jesus as the substance and source of my life. Major Ian Thomas captured it well when he once wrote:

> *The Christian life can be explained only in terms of Jesus, and if your life as a Christian can still be explained in terms of you – your personality, your willpower, your gift, your talent, your money, your courage, your scholarship, your dedication, your sacrifice, or your anything – then although you may have the Christian life, you are not yet living it! ... True Godliness leaves the world convinced beyond a shadow of a doubt that the only explanation for you, is Jesus.*

We are not promoting laziness, apathy, or "sit on a couch until Jesus forces me to do something"; rather, it is my life interacting with His through my surrender, dependency, and response. I become the vessel through which He flows His life, love, gospel, truth, and triumph. I become the stage upon which He acts and demonstrates Himself to this lost and dying world. I become His hands and feet to the needy, broken, and lost.

As Christians, we ought to desire greater growth and depth. It is, as my friend Eric Ludy states, "an endless frontier" to press onward in and explore. As we live in the dark-chocolate richness of intimacy with Jesus in this moment, we realize that this is but a taste and that we must therefore continue onward and upward. Andrew Murray clearly expressed this when he stated:

> *You will ask me, are you satisfied? Have you got all you want? God forbid. With the deepest feeling of my soul I can say that I am satisfied with Jesus now; but there is also the consciousness of how much fuller the revelation can be of the exceeding abundance of His grace. Let us never hesitate to say, This is only the beginning.*

If you want a picture of what such a life looks like, open any biography of the heroic Christians of old, and you will discover a hint of what is possible when we embark down the path of the deeper Christian life.

Below are a few of my favorite "Christian heroes of old."

Some people who lived the Deeper Christian Life throughout the last few centuries

C.T. Studd, Hudson Taylor, Amy Carmichael, George Müller, Rees Howells, Andrew Murray, A.W. Tozer, William and Catherine Booth, Samuel Brengle, Richard Wurmbrand, Major Ian Thomas, Leonard Ravenhill, Corrie ten Boom, Samuel Morris, George Whitefield, John Wesley, David Brainerd, Paris Reidhead, Charles Spurgeon, Francois Fenelon, Watchman Nee, E.M. Bounds, John Hyde, Handley Moule, Jonathan Edwards, Jim and Elisabeth Elliot, Madame Guyon, Keith Green, Jackie Pullinger, D.L. Moody, Charles Trumbull, Gladys Aylward, David Wilkerson, T. Austin-Sparks, Duncan Campbell, Francis Asbury, Jonathan Goforth, and Oswald Chambers.

Simply

Simply put, the Deeper Christian Life is one of absolute surrender to, complete dependency upon, and faithful abiding in Jesus. It is a life that is obsessed with, focused upon, and sourced by Jesus Himself as we live in continual response to Him. Paul said, "I have been crucified with Christ; it is no longer I who live, but Christ lives in me; and the life which I now live in the flesh I live by faith in the Son of God, who loved me and gave Himself for me" (Galatians 2.20).

About NRJohnson

Nathan Johnson (NRJohnson) is a writer, teacher, and communicator who desires to help Christians understand and apply the Bible as they grow and mature in the faith, so that they gain greater intimacy with  Christ, experience the victorious Christian life, and transform the world through the power of the indwelling Holy Spirit.

For more than a decade he has spent his life in a variety of ministry roles, earnest to proclaim Jesus and Him crucified—declaring that the Gospel is more than good news, it is Truth that actually works and has the power to radically transform our lives.

He writes online at **deeperChristian.com**

Special Thanks

Having been a part of the publishing process of over twenty books, I have come to have a greater appreciation for those who are involved in the undertaking.

I am deeply grateful to Stephen Manley for the countless hours he has poured into my life—both as a mentor and as an example of what the Christian life looks like. I first grasped the concept of this book (knowing Jesus) while listening to Stephen preach, and I haven't been the same since.

To the others who have continued to champion this concept in my life: Eric Ludy, Andrew Murray, Major Ian Thomas, Samuel Brengle, Oswald Chambers, AW Tozer, and Leonard Ravenhill—praise Jesus for the testimony of your lives and lasting words.

Practically, a special thank you to Tim Meier, who did the editing, and Mark Carnehl, who helps me in the design department.

And utmost love and thankfulness to Jesus. Oh to know You more!

You will ask me, are you satisfied? Have you got all you want? God forbid. With the deepest feeling of my soul I can say that I am satisfied with Jesus now; but there is also the consciousness of how much fuller the revelation can be of the exceeding abundance of His grace. Let us never hesitate to say, "This is only the beginning."

– Andrew Murray –

Made in the USA
Middletown, DE
10 April 2015